You will always be one
of the people in my life
whom I love the most.
You are the essence of joy
and the true meaning of life.
You are a rare and treasured gift...

You are my beautiful daughter.

~ Linda Sackett-Morrison

Other books in this series...

Blue Mountain Arts®

A Friend Lives in Your Heart Forever

A Mother Is Love

I Love You Soooo Much
by Douglas Pagels

I'd Love to Give These Gifts to You

Keep Believing in Yourself and Your Special Dreams

Promises To Myself

Sister, You Have a Special Place in My Heart

The Greatest Gift of All Is... A Son like You

The Greatest Gift of All Is...

A Daughter
like You

Loving Thoughts from the Heart of a Parent

Blue Mountain Press™
Boulder, Colorado

Library of Congress Catalog Card Number: 2001005403
ISBN: 0-88396-611-5

We wish to thank Susan Polis Schutz for permission to reprint the following poems that appear in this publication: "I love you every minute of every day, my beautiful daughter," "If Ever You Need Someone to Talk to, I Am Always Here for You," "To My Daughter, I Love You," "It Is a Wonderful World, My Daughter... and You Are a Beautiful Part of It," and "Always Believe in Yourself, Daughter." Copyright © 1986, 1991, 1993, 1996 by Stephen Schutz and Susan Polis Schutz. All rights reserved.

ACKNOWLEDGMENTS appear on page 48.

Certain trademarks are used under license.

Manufactured in Thailand.
Fifth Printing: 2003

 This book is printed on recycled paper.

Library of Congress Cataloging-in-Publication Data

The greatest gift of all is — a daughter like you : loving thoughts from the heart of a parent.

    p. cm.

  ISBN 0-88396-611-5 (hardcover : alk. paper)

  1. Mothers and daughters—Poetry. 2. Fathers and daughters—Poetry. 3. Daughters—Poetry.

4. American poetry. I. SPS Studios.

  PS595.M65 G64 2001

  811.008'03520441—dc21

                                   2001005403

                                      CIP

Blue Mountain Arts, Inc.
P.O. Box 4549, Boulder, Colorado 80306

Contents

(Authors listed in order of first appearance)

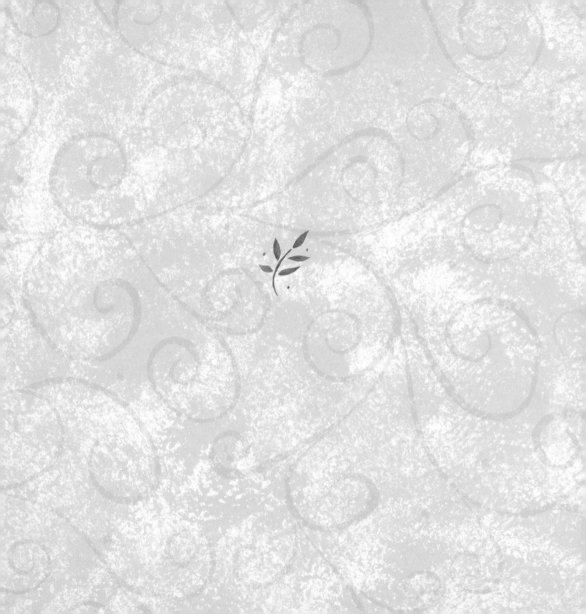

Daughter, as You Make Your Way Through This World, Remember...

There are many experiences you have yet to encounter. I pray that each one, good or bad, will help to mold and shape you, prepare and inspire you, each day of your life.

I don't want you to worry about trials that you may face. Don't think you won't have the strength to endure them, because you will. You have the strength to overcome anything you want. It's only when you start to doubt yourself that you have the potential to fail.

Your dreams are something else I hope you never forget. I want you to wrap your heart around them and never let go. I want you to feel good about them and remind yourself to live with hope.

Make each day yours, and make them all count. Work hard, enjoy yourself, and everything else will somehow seem to fall right where it should. I love you, and I'm very proud of you.

~ T. L. Nash

Thank You, Daughter, for Giving Me Happiness and Smiles

I was thinking about you
and how much you mean to me
and how I can't imagine
    my life without you.
So I decided to share
    these thoughts with you
(even though I hope
    you already know them)...
You are a blessing
that I'm forever thankful for.
I love being with you,
and every time we're apart
there's a little part of me
that stays with you.

Your sense of humor delights me.
Your laughter is one of
    my favorite sounds,
and your smiles light up my heart.
I'm so proud of you
and the kind of person you are.
People know they can count on you.
You go out of your way for others
and make a difference in the lives
    of those you care about.
You're helpful to others,
and you are independent, as well.
I'm very pleased with all
you've accomplished on your own.
I love you, and I want you to know
that being your parent
has been one of my greatest joys.

~ Barbara Cage

I love you every minute of every day, my beautiful daughter

I looked at you today
and saw the same beautiful eyes
that looked at me with love
when you were a baby
I looked at you today
and saw the same beautiful mouth
that made me cry when you first smiled at me
when you were a baby
It was not long ago
that I held you in my arms
long after you fell asleep
and I just kept rocking you
all night long

I looked at you today
and saw my beautiful daughter
no longer a baby
but a beautiful person
with a full range of emotions and feelings
and ideas and goals
Every day is exciting
as I continue to watch you grow
And I want you to always know that
in good and in bad times
I will love you
and that no matter what you do
or how you think
or what you say
you can depend on
my support, guidance
friendship and love
every minute of every day
I love being your mother

~ Susan Polis Schutz

I'm Proud of the Woman You Are

When you were young,
I thought of your future life.
Perhaps you would fly to the moon
Or, if not, at least land on a star.
I knew you could do whatever
You set your mind to.
I saw you as a leader,
Strong in your convictions,
Able to move mountains not
Just for yourself,
But also able to move obstacles
out of others' paths.
I am so proud of you,
Of the woman you have become
With all your effort and hard work.
I hope you can feel
The warm love I have for you
Today and always.

~ Carol Lawson

Sweet Daughter of Mine...

Did you know
That my world changed forever
When you came into my life?
No one could have prepared me
For the depth of love
That sprang into my heart for you
From the very moment you were born.
It seems that every day
I think of ways I can let you know
How very special you are to me.
You truly are a treasure,
And I will cherish you all my life.
I will brag about you and show you off
Every time I get the chance.
And though I don't know how it's possible,
You become more dear to me
With every year that passes by.

~ Cheryl Barker

Daughter, You Are
the Light of My Life

The day you came into my life
a star dropped from the sky
and lit a flame inside my heart
Watching you grow
that light burned brighter
fueled by pride in each of your
   accomplishments
and by the greatest love
for all that you have become
This flame keeps me going
It comforts my soul and
   completes my life
knowing that I have blessed the world
with the most precious of gifts

You have made your place in this world
    so quickly
discovering your independence
and becoming your own beautiful person
I want you to know always
that no matter the time that passes
    between us
no matter the distance separating our hearts
my heart will be filled with the light
you sparked so many years ago
and it will continue to burn
so that you will always feel
the love and comfort of home
    and never feel alone

~ Deana Marino

Wishes for You,
Daughter

I wish you love and happiness
Perfect health your whole life through
As much money as you need
   to make life easier
To do the things you want to

I wish you joy and satisfaction
The appreciation you so deserve
Courage when you're fearful
When you're about to lose your nerve

I wish you good friends to call on
A playful heart to keep you young
Special memories to hold on to
Pretty melodies to be sung

I hope you have someone to talk to
And to be with when you please
To share life's special things with
Like a walk among the trees

To share a blanket in the wintertime
To protect you from the cold
To picnic with in the summertime
To hug and kiss and hold

Remember, things may not always work out
    for the best in life
But you can make the best of everything
Just turn those lessons from your journey
Into songs that you can sing

If I could package up my love for you
With a ribbon and a bow
Whatever you want would be yours
    for the asking
Whatever you need, wherever you go

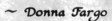

~ Donna Fargo

You're a Wonderful Daughter

I want you to know of some
special feelings that I carry with me
in my heart all the time.

The feelings are about how much
I cherish you. How proud I am of you.
How many hopes and dreams I want
to come true for you.
    And how happy I want you to be.

Even during some of our heart~to~heart talks,
the words I want to say don't always get said.
But the feelings are felt. Always.

You're a special person... all your own.
    But as you grow and learn and change
        with the days, I want you to know
        of one thing that will never change.
And that... is my endless love... for you.

~ Laurel Atherton

If Ever You Need Someone to Talk to, I Am Always Here for You

If ever things are not
going well for you
and you have some problems to solve
If ever you are feeling confused
and don't know the right thing to do
If ever you are feeling frightened
and hurt
or if you just need someone
to talk to
please remember that
I am here for you at all times
without judgment
and with understanding
and love

~ Susan Polis Schutz

Everything I Do as Your Parent, I Do Out of Love for You

You probably can't imagine the love
    parents have for their children,
But you need to know that it is
    constant and unconditional.
Nothing can change it, and it
    never, ever goes away.
A parent's love is there through the
    discipline and the disagreements;
It's in every action and every decision.
Unfortunately, it isn't always
    apparent or obvious,
And sometimes parents make mistakes
    or wrong decisions.
We try to do what is best and fair,
    but we don't always get it right.
Emotions, moods, fear, and love
    get in the way.

A fierce desire to keep our children safe
Often causes us to say "no" when
    you are begging for a "yes."
Parents must keep the past and future
    in mind with each choice they make,
Knowing that children often see only the "now"
And are not always aware of consequences
    and temptations.
Our goal is to help you become all you can be
So that you are safe and happy now
And can live a fulfilling and successful life
    in the future.
Hopefully, someday you'll understand,
But until then, know that you are a
    special person ~
One who is precious, cherished, and
    most of all... loved.

~ Barbara Cage

My Promises to You, Daughter

When you are happy,
I'll love you with
a joyful heart.
When you are sad,
I'll love you with a heart
made a little heavier
by your tears.

When you are right,
I'll love you with a heart
filled with pride.
When you are wrong,
I'll love you with a heart
that has learned acceptance.
When you succeed,
I'll love you with a cheering heart.

When you fail,
I'll love you with a heart
that rewards the efforts
you've made.
When you dream,
I'll love you with
an encouraging heart.
When you give up,
I'll love you with a heart
that is strong enough
for both of us.
When you are simply you,
in whatever mood or phase of your life,
I'll love you with all my heart
and more than you'll ever know.

~ Linda Sackett~Morrison

Remember, Daughter...
You Are Someone Special

Everyone is unique and different. Appreciate your own uniqueness and realize that you're an angel in disguise to some, a friend so important to others, and a member of a family with whom you have significance and importance beyond description.

May the love in your life, hope in your heart, and faith in your dreams help you to do whatever will make you happy, keep you healthy, and assure you the prosperity you deserve.

May the joy and peace and blessings in your life help you change something that you want or need to change and accept something that perhaps you haven't been able to change and just need to accept.

May you find satisfaction in your work and all the other things that make your day-to-day life more balanced and content and rewarding. May you have happiness in your family, unconditional love for one another, and understanding. May you tap into the capacity and knowledge to embrace the gift of love that dwells in your heart and that is replenished when given away.

Special people are the ones who change our lives, make us feel good about ourselves, and help us believe it's possible to realize our dreams. They give us a sense of community and belonging. They make us feel appreciated and accepted and move us toward our own emotional security. May you always remember that... you are someone special.

~ Donna Fargo

The best feeling in this world is family.
From it, we draw love,
friendship, moral support,
and the fulfillment of every
special need within our hearts.
In a family, we are connected to
an ever-present source
of sunny moments, smiles and laughter,
understanding and encouragement,
and hugs that help us grow in confidence
all along life's path.
Wherever we are, whatever we're doing,
whenever we really need to feel
especially loved, befriended, supported,
and cared for in the greatest way,
our hearts can turn to the family
and find the very best
always waiting for us.

~ Barbara J. Hall

A Family's Love Can Rise Above Anything That Comes Along

*M*y dear and wonderful daughter,
we all have times
when it seems like
the sun forgot to shine in our lives
and the dreams we were counting
so heavily on... forgot how much
we wanted them to come true.

When you need a place of comfort,
a hand to hold, and a heart that cares
about your happiness more than words
can ever say... remember that you can
turn to me... and I'll do whatever
I can to help you
    chase those clouds away.

~ Ann Turrel

To My Daughter, I Love You

So many times
you ask me questions
and your big beautiful eyes
look at me
with trust, confusion and
innocence
I always hope that my
answers to you
will help guide you
Even though I always want to protect you
and step in for you when you have a
   difficult decision to make
it is very important that I do not interfere
so that you will learn from your own experiences
and develop confidence in your own judgment

There is a fine line between
a mother telling her daughter
too much
or too little
I hope I have struck a proper balance
I have always wanted to tell you
how honored I am that you
seek out my opinions
I appreciate the trust you have in me and
I want you to know that
I have an immense trust in you
I am very proud of you
as I watch you growing up to be an
intelligent, independent, sensitive young woman
I love you

~ Susan Polis Schutz

Wherever You May Go in Life, Daughter, My Love Goes with You

There are so many things
   I want to say to you,
so many thoughts and feelings
   I want to leave with you,
as you venture out into a world
   of your own making.
I don't know how I can possibly
   express them all.
I want you to know, first of all,
   how much I love you and how proud
      I am of you.
You are, without a doubt, one of the best
   things that has ever happened to me.
Wherever you go in life,
   whatever you choose to do,
I know you'll accomplish greatness.

If you are ever in doubt about anything,
just trust your intuition and go with your
      best judgment, because no one
knows you better than you know yourself.
Don't worry if you make a mistake
      or change your direction from time to time;
you still have many more "learning" years
      ahead of you.
And if you ever need help or advice or
      just someone to talk to,
I'll always be here for you in any way
      that I can be.

Perhaps most important of all,
I want to thank you...
      for all the smiles and good times,
      for the opportunity to share
            your life's experiences,
      for the friendship we now share,
      and for being the best daughter
            anyone could ever ask for.

~ Anna Marie Edwards

Keep Reaching for the Stars, Dear Daughter

Day by day, year by year
I've watched you grow
grabbing hold of life
with grace and determination
making it your own
molding your dreams into reality
I've watched as you fill to the brim
with happiness and pride
with each new accomplishment
I have seen your heart broken
and felt your pain
as the tears spilled from your eyes
I know the sadness that consumes you
when those who are supposed to care
belittle your ambition
trying to take control
of your destiny

I've seen traces of doubt
begin to invade
tearing at your self~confidence
and I begin to worry
that maybe this time
you won't heal
But after allowing yourself
to feel the pain
to cry the tears
you do heal
Stronger and more determined
you tighten your grip on life
leaving the negative behind
I gladly share all this with you
My daughter
you are a survivor
and you fill me with pride

~ Sharon M. McCabe

It Is a Wonderful World,
My Daughter... and You Are
a Beautiful Part of It

The world was made
to be beautiful ~
but sometimes we get caught up in
everyday actions
completely forgetting about this
completely forgetting that
what is truly important
are the simple, basic things in life ~
honest, pure emotions
surrounded by the majestic beauty of nature
We need to concentrate on
the freeness and peacefulness of nature
and not on the driven material aspects of life
We need to smell the clear air
after the rainfall
and appreciate the good in things

Each of us must be responsible
and do our part
in order to help preserve a beautiful world ~
the waterfalls, the oceans, the mountains
the large gray boulders
the large green farms
the fluffy pink clouds
the sunrises and sunsets, ladybugs
rainbows, dew, hummingbirds
butterflies, dandelions
We need to remember that
we are here for a short time
and that every day should count for something
and that every day we should be thankful
for all the natural beauty
The world is a wonderful place
and we are so lucky to be a part of it

~ Susan Polis Schutz

My Love for You
Has a Lifetime Guarantee

You are the sparkle in my eyes and the pride in my heart. You are the courage that gives me strength and the love that gives me life. You are my inspiration and the best gift I ever received.

Maybe I don't always show it, but I love you with every beat of my heart. Maybe I don't always tell you, but no words can express what you mean to me. I pray that I've always done right by you; believe me, I've tried my best.

No matter where life's path takes you or the difficulties you may encounter, know that I'm with you in spirit. My love has a lifetime guarantee. If ever you're in trouble or just need a friend, I'm no further away than a phone call. You are my child, and I feel so blessed that I am allowed to be a part of your life.

~ Lois Carruthers

Daughter, Here Are Some Things I Want You to Know and Remember...

Please know and remember that it is with the greatest joy that I am your guardian, protector, and nurturer.

Please know and remember that I will always strive to fulfill these roles with honor, trust, and respect for your thoughts, feelings, and individuality.

What matters most in life are the people you love, and, for always, you will be one of the people in my life whom I love the most.

You are the essence of joy and the true meaning of life.

You are the part of me that I'm most proud of because you're you.

You are a rare and treasured gift.

You are a dream with all its hope and promise.

You are love, endless and pure.

You are my beautiful daughter.

Please know and remember this, always.

~ Linda Sackett-Morrison

To My Amazing Daughter...

"Look at you!" These words spill out
when you surprise me, standing there
  looking so grown~up and lovely.
I feel as if I'm seeing you for the
  very first time.
These same words spill out when you
  catch me off~guard
with your success out in a
  fast-paced world,
turning your childhood dreams
  into realities,
and when you awe me with your
  unexpected strength of heart

and wisdom far beyond your years,
astounding me with the person
  you have become.

"Look at you!" These words come out
when I'm really talking to myself,
telling the parent in me to wake up
and see this amazing young woman
standing where I left my baby girl.
But I'm not only reminding myself to look,
I'm also reminding you, as well ~
to know how very special you are,
to see your value, your true worth,
reflected in my eyes.
I have always loved you, dearest child,
just as you were and
    as I knew you'd become ~
but seeing the reality amazes me.
Now I want most for you to
    "Look at you!"
and to truly love what you see.

~ Beth Thompson

A Daughter Is Forever

A daughter is one of the greatest blessings
  one could ever have
She begins her life loving and trusting you
  automatically
For many years, you are the center of her life
Together you experience the delights of
  the new things she learns and does
You enter into a daughter's play and are once
  again young
And even though it's harder to enter into her
  world as she becomes a teen...
You are there, understanding her dilemmas and
  her fears
And wishing with all your heart that she
  didn't have to go through them
A daughter's smile is a precious sight that
  you treasure each time you see it
And the sound of her laughter always brings
  joy to your heart

Her successes mean more to you than your own
And her happiness is your happiness
Her heartaches and disappointments
  become yours, too
Because when she isn't okay, you can't
  be okay either
Daughters aren't perfect
  but you, Daughter, come close to it
You have given me more happiness
  than you know
I am thankful for your kindness and thoughtfulness
And I am proud of who you are
  and how you live your life
Words can't express how much you mean to me
  or how much I love you
The love goes too deep, and the gratitude
  and pride I feel are boundless
Thank you for blessing my life
  in so many ways

~ Barbara Cage

Dear Daughter of Mine...

Through the years, I watched you grow, change, and constantly question everything. When you were little, there was an overwhelming feeling inside me that wanted to hold you close and keep you safe and warm all your life. Yet as the years passed, I realized that I couldn't do that. You have always been a child full of wonder, and to keep you so close to me would have deprived you of experiencing life's wonders.

Now, after years of letting you go your own way and watching you become a beautiful young lady, our roles have changed. You are still my daughter and I am still your parent, but most precious of all is the fact that we have become good friends, and we have a friendship that will stand the test of time.

I want you to know that I'll always cherish the wonder and joy of watching you grow into a beautiful young lady. I'll always be proud to say, "This is my daughter." But most of all, I'm proud to say that you are my best friend.

~ Vicky Lafleur

Always Believe in Yourself, Daughter
...and Know that You Are Loved

Know yourself ~
what you can do
and want to do in life
Set goals
and work hard to achieve them
Have fun every day in every way
Be creative ~
it is an expression of your feelings
Be sensitive in viewing the world
Believe in the family
as a stable and rewarding way of life
Believe in love
as the most complete
and important emotion possible
Believe that you are
an important part of
everyone's life that you touch
Believe in yourself
and know that you are loved

~ Susan Polis Schutz

You Are a Wonderful Daughter

I have asked myself
   (as every parent does)
if I have loved you enough
and done the very best job
   that I could for you.
Then, as human nature goes,
   I remember mistakes
      that I made
and how they might have hurt you.
Yet I never stopped loving you,
   even in the times
      when I seemed distant.

I am so proud that you are my child;
when I think of you,
     I feel tears in my eyes
because you make me so happy.
I wonder why I haven't told you this
     much more often than I have,
but sometimes it's hardest to say
     what we feel strongest about.
So I don't want to let
     another moment pass
without telling you
how much you mean to me
and how very much I love you.

~ Linda Hersey

Daughter, You Are
Life's Greatest Gift to Me

Memories come flooding back to me
   as I look back over the years.
I want to hold on to you
   and at the same time
watch you fly high and free.

You have such spirit and a character
   all your own.
You are a doer, and an achiever
   of what you believe in.
I'm so proud of your dreams
   and the conviction you have
to make those dreams come true.
Your world is bright, new,
   and bursting with possibilities.

It's so easy to remember
   your very first steps
and how I held out my hand
   for you to hold.
As each year passes
   you take more steps,
and some of these will eventually
   lead you away from me ~
but always remember that my hand
   and my heart are forever here for you.
You will always be my daughter,
   but I have also discovered in you
a rare and precious friend.
You have been life's greatest gift to me,
and I love you so much.

~ Vickie M. Worsham

ACKNOWLEDGMENTS

The following is a partial list of authors whom the publisher especially wishes to thank for permission to reprint their works.

T. L. Nash for "Daughter, as You Make Your Way Through This World, Remember…." Copyright © 2002 by T. L. Nash. All rights reserved.

PrimaDonna Entertainment Corp. for "Wishes for You, Daughter" and "Remember, Daughter… You Are Someone Special" by Donna Fargo. Copyright © 1999, 2000 by PrimaDonna Entertainment Corp. All rights reserved.

Barbara Cage for "Everything I Do as Your Parent, I Do Out of Love for You." Copyright © 2002 by Barbara Cage. All rights reserved.

Beth Thompson for "To My Amazing Daughter…." Copyright © 2002 by Beth Thompson. All rights reserved.

A careful effort has been made to trace the ownership of poems used in this anthology in order to obtain permission to reprint copyrighted materials and give proper credit to the copyright owners. If any error or omission has occurred, it is completely inadvertent, and we would like to make corrections in future editions provided that written notification is made to the publisher:

BLUE MOUNTAIN ARTS, INC., P.O. Box 4549, Boulder, Colorado 80306.